NOTES FROM T̶H̶E̶ ̶D̶E̶S̶K̶ OF AN UNEXPECTED CHIEF

STOPPING
RELATIONSHIP VIOLENCE
ONE COP'S EXPERIENCE

BY LARRY RINEHART

Copyright

First Published by Metcalf Design & Printing Center, Gahanna, Ohio
Copyright 2002, 2003, 2004, 2005, 2006, 2007, 2008

Copyright 2012 by Larry Rinehart
Stopping Relationship Violence - One Cop's Experience
ISBN-13: 978-1469964881
ISBN-10: 1469964880

WORD SPIGOT PUBLISHING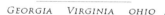

GEORGIA   VIRGINIA   OHIO

Cover design and layout by Phyllis Stewart
Phyllis can be contacted at pstewart0831@sbcglobal.net

Printed in the USA

Dedication

This book is dedicated to Laura, Lindsey, Elizabeth and all those who have suffered at the hand of an abuser.

Preface

"Family violence - don't pass it on."
-P.E.A.C.E. Initiative

You don't know what woke you from the sound sleep, but your heart is racing and as you become wide awake, you hear loud, violent noise. Your bedroom is on the second floor of the house and you realize the noise and loud voices are coming from downstairs. You look over at the alarm clock and see it is just after 2:30 in the morning. Your heart is still racing, but there is a familiar ring to the violent struggle just one floor below where you lay. Now you notice the flashing police lights coming through your bedroom window and wonder how long they have been there. You pray the violence does not reach your room as you pull the covers over your head. You are eight years old.

Relationship violence is a plague on our society that crosses every ethnic, racial, religious and economic boundary. In many families violence is a way of life that perpetuates itself, generation after generation. Just today I read an article in The Columbus Dispatch citing a seven-year study of several hundred Springfield, Massachusetts kids. One conclusion of the study was that youth violence has its deepest roots in excessively violent households as opposed to poverty, gender and race as previously thought.

They could have asked any cop that question and saved the cost of the study.

As the Chief of Police of a suburban police department bordering Columbus, Ohio, and as a public speaker, I have talked to thousands of kids and adults about relationship violence and its cycle. I have great passion for the subject, having experienced relationship violence on many different levels in my own life.

As a police officer, I have been in far too many homes where the violence is alive and well. Usually, it is mom and dad doing the fighting while the next generation of fighters sit in the corner and watch or lie in their beds and listen. In almost every community officers respond to domestic violence calls every day. Police officers will tell you that it's not the size of the house, cost of the car in the drive, or color of skin that determines which families are caught in the cycle. Not surprisingly, substance abuse is often involved, but not always. It is the background of the family member that typically makes this determination.

It was suggested to me that I write down the words of my presentation and share it with those who may never hear my words. The following is my best attempt to capture not only the words, but also the passion of my presentation. I wrote this booklet in 2001, not long after the death of my sister, Laura.

Since that time I have had the opportunity to work with and support several anti-violence nonprofit organizations in the Columbus, Ohio area. I have also provided speaking presentations for many other Domestic Violence organizations around the state, usually during their annual meetings or domestic violence awareness month. I am always amazed at the dedication and perseverance of the hard working (and usually underpaid) employees who staff those critical nonprofit organizations. They staff crisis hotlines, provide counseling, act as advocates often when the victims have no one else to stand by them in their time of desperate need. They provide emergency shelter in the middle of the night when victims are forced to make their escape from violence. These advocates, some paid and some volunteer, save lives every day.

As I write this I am honored to serve as president of the board of directors for "CHOICES, Eliminating Domestic Violence." CHOICES is in it's 35th year of serving central Ohio by operating the Franklin County battered victim's shelter, the 24 hour crisis hotline and providing many other victim services.

Much has changed in my life since 2001. I have changed jobs, moving about 15 minutes down the road to become the police chief of a tremendous community and working with some of the finest law enforcement professionals I have ever known. My son is almost 21 years old and growing into a fine talented young man. My daughter and son-in-law have blessed me with three beautiful, happy and healthy granddaughters. And of course, my two nieces have grown up, graduated from high school, and are working to find their way in this life as they deal with a tragedy that no person should have to deal with.

I have also given more presentations and participated in more panel discussions than I can remember in my efforts as an advocate against family violence. I tell women, young and old, to know the warning signs of a potentially harmful relationship and to know when to get out and when to call the police. I tell young men that the vast majority of the time men are the problem. We cannot treat women as though they are our property, we need to control our rage. When the relationship is over, it is over. Aggressive, possessive, stalking, and violent behavior is not acceptable in a civilized society.

One thing that has not changed is the scope of the problem. Relationship and family violence still terrorizes a large part of our society. As a rule, whenever I give my presentation, women approach me afterwards to tell me of their own personal experiences with an abuser. Any time I speak to a group of five or more, someone in the group has been scarred by an abuser. It never fails. For every woman who tells me her story, I know there are many more women still trapped in abusive relationships.

Relationship violence transcends all social, racial, and economic groups. It is not a "poor-people" problem and it is not just a problem for any one particular race. Many men learned their abuse tactics from watching their fathers and many more men simply don't care to control their rage. Shockingly, many men believe it is a sign of strength and power to control and abuse the women in their lives, physically and emotionally. And, all too often it starts at a very young age.

So, we advocates keep speaking out and continue to spread the word to our daughters, nieces, mothers, friends, coworkers, fellow students and to any group willing to gather to listen. The abused must escape the violence and abusers must stop the cycle of violence.

In closing I need to send an overdue thank you to Mrs. Linda Shannon, a health teacher at Gahanna-Lincoln High School and an all around great lady. Early in 2001

Linda prompted me to tell my story for the first time to her health students. She will remember that as I stood in front of them trying to put the story into some logical format, I became sweat soaked and struggled. But, that is where my advocacy began. We've come a long way since that beginning.

-*Larry Rinehart*
January 2012

Introduction

*"Have you ever felt afraid of someone
who loves you?"*
-Coalition Against Domestic Violence Billboard

When I speak to groups about relationship violence, many people automatically think about domestic violence. Over the past several years there has been much talk and media discussion about domestic violence and many people think the legal system sufficiently addresses the issue. Unfortunately, this is not always the case.

The Ohio Revised Code (ORC) fully explains the law that covers domestic violence. It is very specific in speaking to violence or threats of violence committed by a "family or household member." While this covers acts of violence between people who live together, it fails to address the issue of relationship violence.

In my presentations I speak of violence on a much broader scale. Simply put, I address the violence that people commit or fall victim to with someone they are having, or have had, a relationship with. Most high school kids don't live with the people they date or hang out with. Relationship violence is much bigger than the ORC definition of domestic violence. However, growing up in a domestic violence household is often at the core of the relationship violence we allow to sneak into our lives.

I first became interested in the area of Relationship Violence as a new patrol officer assigned to activities that took me around the local high school, Gahanna Lincoln. I was intrigued by the growing trend where high school-age boys would talk down to their girlfriends in front of their buddies. It had somehow become cool for boys to call their girlfriends degrading names like "bitch" and "whore" to gain the respect of their male counterparts. I even observed incidents where boys would grab and to a degree "manhandle" their girlfriends. More intriguing was the fact that many high school girls not only accepted the abuse, but also seemed to tolerate it as some type of a badge of toughness. I couldn't believe it.

Keep in mind that I'm not talking about a rough and tumble inner-city school where one has to accept abuse to survive, the kind most of us see in the movies. This is Gahanna Lincoln, an upper-middle class, suburban school where there are many nicer cars in the parking lot than a lot of working people can afford. In fact, one of the biggest community problems each school year is where the kids can park their cars since the school parking lot overfills quickly. Most of the kids I am talking about come from affluent, beautiful suburban homes, structurally speaking.

The Cycle of Relationship Violence

"He hits me. He hits me not. He hits me.
He hits me not. He hits me . . ."
-Thaw Studio Billboard, 2009

As a police officer that responded to many domestic violence calls and now as a police administrator who hears the volume of domestic violence calls and often reviews police reports, I know many kids grow up in violent homes. The violence ranges in degree and duration, but I believe most kids see it at some point. Maybe mom or dad spanks the kids too often and too hard or maybe the kids get slapped when they become a nuisance. Maybe someone drinks a little too much occasionally and hits a wall or worse. Maybe there is a lot of shouting, even swearing and threatening. Or maybe dad simply beats mom once in a while. I believe few households are completely exempt. I believe many of these scenarios are happening every week in our neighborhoods and the kids are watching and learning.

There are a few different versions of the "Domestic Violence Wheel." I use a basic model, which is just as appropriate for relationship violence as it is for domestic violence. First, the "Honeymoon Period." For most households and relationships this is the time everyone is in love and getting along. This is the period of tranquility that most of us live for and a time of peace. For the most dysfunctional relationships, this may simply be a time of tolerance, a time when no one is being hurt. Either way, this is the best period in the house or relationship where things are as good as they get.

Next comes the "Tension Building Period." Many things can lead to this period: a bad day, loss of a job, substance abuse issues, and unresolved issues from previous arguments, etc. Some of us are simply programmed to instigate this period whether we know it or not. Regardless of the reason, it is clear to everyone we are leaving the honeymoon period and what lies ahead is not good.

Finally comes the "Explosion." This is when it all blows up. The argument leads to shoving or pushing or worse. It is during this period that people punch holes in walls, and in worst cases, try to punch holes in each other. Often substance abuse is involved. Maybe someone stopped by the local watering hole on the way home, but not always. The degree of violence in this period varies greatly, anywhere from a heated discussion in more functional relationships and households to near-murder in much more dysfunctional homes. To a blessed few of us, this violent period is a foreign concept and hard to believe. Believe me, this violent period is played out in almost every community, every day.

Some families have lived in the cycle for so long that they fully realize the honeymoon period is only temporary. The kids are usually the ones who know what is to come. They tell their friends, "Yeah, things are cool now, but it is only a matter of time before it blows up again." The close friends of the kids become familiar with the cycle. Often kids come home from school or a friend's house, see that one parent is drinking and decide to make themselves scarce in order to avoid the inevitable blow up. It probably happens in your neighborhood, maybe just down the street. Affluent families are good at hiding the dysfunction. Don't think that just because you don't see it, it isn't happening.

Maybe you have seen it in your neighborhood and maybe you have lived it in your home or relationships. One thing is for certain, many people live much of their lives locked into this cycle and it rarely ever changes. In some cases people live their entire lives in this cycle. Many people grow up in this cycle and go on to perpetuate it in their adult lives. Regardless, in my experience, nothing short of a significant emotional event can break the cycle.

A Significant Emotional Event and the Law

"Well, he said he was sorry."
-A friend

Many people ask for the definition of "a significant emotional event." There is no single, exact, specific event that does it for everyone. For a rare few relationship violence offenders, a single trip to jail is a life-changing event, but for most it is not enough. For an even rarer few, simply having the police knock on their door after a 911 call is enough. For many, watching their victim lay in a hospital bed during a lengthy recovery from the physical violence does not change their behavior. I suspect the most effective, behavior changing "significant emotional event" is first, an admission of the problem and a strong desire to make the change and second, long term counseling, not unlike the recovery required for an alcoholic.

Over the past several years the Domestic Violence law has changed significantly in Ohio. When I first came to the Gahanna PD in 1994, officers had a great amount of discretion in how they handled domestic violence calls. For instance, in most domestic violence situations an argument escalates to physical violence, usually the husband or boyfriend becomes physical with the wife or girlfriend. In a few rare cases it is the other way around. When the fight reaches fever pitch, the peak of the violence period, somebody calls the police, often the wife, a neighbor, or the kids. More often than not, by the time the police arrive, the fight is over.

In my presentations I ask people when they believe the relationship moves from the violence stage back to the honeymoon period. I hear a range of answers. The truth is, quite often the sales pitch for the honeymoon period begins right after the person who became violent realizes the police have been called. The pitch goes something like this, "Honey, I am so sorry I shoved/hit/hurt you. You know I love you. It's just that I have been under so much pressure lately because of my job/health/bad luck, etc. Please forgive me. I swear this will never happen again." In some repeat cases he may even promise to seek help, if only she will forgive him.

And of course, what period are we all looking for? We're looking for the honeymoon period. In domestic relationships it is usually the wife that does the forgiving because she is anxious to get back to the honeymoon period. Who can blame her? Consider the options.

She can have the husband or boyfriend arrested only to have him back on her doorstep in a couple days, if that long. If she does find a way to be rid of him, the financial impact could be devastating, especially when there are children involved and she has already sacrificed her career options to raise the kids. And what about the cases where she still really loves the guy? She might not want him gone, just violence free. Many victims live in denial, believing that this time things will be different, but they rarely are.

It is right about now that I remind my audience of two things, especially when I am talking with high school kids. First, I tell the boys that even though I most often refer to the violent person as he or him, I am not male bashing. I am a member of that brotherhood. The truth is, in our culture 95% of victims are female. I remember a few cases where this was not true, but by and large the men in our society do the beating. It is not male bashing. It is the ugly truth.

Second, many kids who live in the home I just described think they are trapped. They become desperate and feel like there is no way out. They know that even though mom and dad/boyfriend just made up again, it is only a matter of time before the next blow up. Just because the parents are in denial doesn't mean the kids are.

I tell them they are not trapped. Regardless of the home they live in, they will grow up and out of it. They will have their opportunity to move on and achieve all their dreams.

However, I tell them that if they don't take steps to prevent it, they could easily wake up some day and find themselves in the exact same dysfunctional relationship and household they are in now. Only now, they are the adults. And, without a significant emotional event to break the cycle, they really are trapped.

So, the violence period is over, the husband or boyfriend pleads his case, usually the wife gives in and it is about that time that the police knock on the door; "Police, open up. We received a 911 call," or something similar to that.

As I said, the law has changed. Used to be that unless the victim was willing to sign charges immediately, the police would not take action. That's right, even if there were obvious signs of a struggle and maybe even signs of physical contact (scratches or redness, etc.). In worse case scenarios, the police might talk one person into leaving for a while or maybe even the night "to let things cool down a bit." But that was it.

Police, myself being one of them, liked this option. Sure, we were the world's biggest enablers, but the alternative was a mound of paperwork, tons of time facilitating an arrest, trying to sort out who was at fault, and probably a court appearance later where the victim would often recant her entire testimony of the evening of the incident. It was a heck of a lot easier to calm the situation, de-escalate tempers, maybe even conduct some hip-pocket counseling and leave, usually without as much as a police report being taken.

Cops walked away from these situations all the time feeling like they had really accomplished something. They had not only stopped the violence, however temporarily, but they had taken the opportunity to "power-counsel" the adults, especially the person they believed to be the instigator, usually the man. Again, without a significant emotional event the cycle continued. As I said, for most households and relationships caught up in this cycle, having the police knock on the door and talk for a while is not a significant emotional event. It simply becomes part of the process.

Someone realized that this type of response was doing absolutely nothing to help the families caught up in the domestic violence cycle. Someone realized that allowing this cycle to continue was only perpetuating the problem, generation after generation. Someone noticed that the police were returning to the same households over and over again, in spite of their efforts to keep a lid on the violence. The lid kept blowing off. Often the violence escalated. Someone noticed that multiple police responses for domestic violence at the same residences had not stopped some women from being murdered. The law changed.

Current Ohio law requires officers to take action or document completely their choice not to take action. The victim no longer needs to sign or file charges against the person who was violent to them. The police are required to do that. Where there are signs of physical violence or where there is a credible witness, the police must make an arrest. When both parties are guilty, both parties are arrested. The arrested party spends the night in jail and cannot post bond on the first night. They must appear in front of a judge. This gives the victim some time to acquire a protection order. Victims are provided with a handbook describing different social agencies that can help them. At least at our department, officers no longer get out of taking the paper. If police officers don't take the appropriate action and the victim is hurt further, the police officer assumes the liability. Talk about an incentive to take action.

This new law is not perfect and I am told that the farther one gets away from a major metropolitan area, the looser the interpretation and enforcement. After the initial change in the law, the courts were swamped, literally overloaded, but they seem to have adjusted. We have also seen the creation of better social and volunteer organizations to address the issues of family and relationship violence.

As I said, the law is not perfect, but at least society is addressing the problem. Domestic violence and dispute runs are still up, but at least people are given more opportunities to seek solutions. As a side note, I hear more dispatched runs these days where the violent person is a son or daughter. Used to be it was always mom and dad. Things seem to be changing a bit.

The Path of Tolerance

"I came to know when he was approaching a
period of rage.
I could recognize the signs and would adjust my
behavior accordingly.
It became like a dance."
-*Anonymous victim of a violent marriage*

When I speak to young people, I try hard to make two major points, which are the crux of my message. First, I speak candidly to the women in the audience about what I call "the path of tolerance." Second, I speak to the entire group about how our past tends to program us even when we don't want it to.

I believe one reason high school age girls tolerate the macho type abuse that I spoke of earlier from their boyfriends is because they don't see the danger in it. Maybe they even get caught up in the machismo a bit themselves. It is popular in many affluent suburbs for kids to play the part of the rough and tumble, disadvantaged, angry urban youth they often see portrayed on TV or in the movies. Police officers often interact with "at risk youths" several times before the police get the opportunity to meet the parents or visit the home.

It is common for police to buy into the portrayed image of the street smart, angry, disadvantaged youth only to find out that the kid actually comes from a high-income family living in a high-income area. Often, the parents are oblivious to the role their kid is trying to play. Some kids go to great lengths to play the role, including carrying guns and becoming involved in drugs. Mom and dad are often career professionals and simply not around a lot. Junior is left to his own defenses. Mom and dad mistake providing their kids with "the land of plenty" for responsible parenting. The two don't automatically go together and are often at odds with each other.

The common scenario is this: the kid gets into trouble, maybe a minor scuffle, experimental drug use, disorderly conduct, or even worse. The police track down the parents and explain what's been going on. It still amazes me how many parents become defensive and refuse to believe that junior could be playing out such a role. For many cops, the police officer perspective is that the higher level of income, the higher level of denial and defensiveness. The police, and often school administrators, become the enemy. Junior tells mom that the police are making it up and he is not getting a fair deal. Mom and dad often, not always, side with junior and add enabling to the poor parenting list of denial and defensiveness. It is simply incredible. But I digress.

I watch some young girls buy right into the angry youth role, abuse and all. The problem is, once they take the first step down the path of tolerance it can quickly become a way of life. I plead with young women to not take that first step and to never accept anything less than 100% respect from the boys they date or hang around with.

The path of tolerance is a slippery slope and in worse case scenarios can lead to a life of violence or worse.

Some girls and women don't like the abuse and even become angered by it, as they should. But, for many reasons they stay in the relationship. Maybe the guy is really popular or maybe he is really a great friend when his buddies are not around. Maybe she really loves him and thinks she can change him or he will just change on his own. Maybe he provides something she can't find anywhere else: love, companionship, money, popularity, etc. Whatever the reason, they take abuse from name calling to rough physical contact. It amazes me, but I still see it at every high school football game I attend.

I tell young women that if they ever experience any type of violence from their boyfriends or with the boys they hang out with, to cut off the relationship immediately. Don't look back. End it and get on with their life. If the guy keeps bugging them, call the police. Ohio has solid menacing and stalking laws. Make it clear to him and his family, if necessary, that the relationship is over. Leave him to fix his own problems. Don't take any ownership or responsibility for his dysfunction. It is his problem and he can fix it and find another girlfriend, period. That is the only way. I also tell high school girls to brief their family on the experience. They need to know that Junior has some issues and is no longer welcome in her life. I don't know how successful this middle-aged cop is at getting through to high school kids, but if I reach one I have been successful.

Programming

"Generally, domestic violence occurs when an abuser has learned the behavior and chooses to abuse."
-Choices

My second major point is the way we become programmed. I tell my audiences that I realize some of them grew up in perfect households where everyone loved each other and every relationship was and remains completely functional. I believe there are some homes like that somewhere. I have never personally known of a single one. I ask the kids to raise their hand if they live in a home like that. No one has ever seriously raised his or her hand. Generation gap and all, at this point I always have their attention. By this place in the presentation I have talked to at least one point that they have personal knowledge of or experience with.

I tell them I am speaking to the people who grew up in, or currently live in, something less than a "Brady Bunch" type home. I firmly believe the vast majority of homes have some level of dysfunction. This dysfunction can range from a lack of good communication to a substance abuse ridden, violent household. Many kids live more towards the later.

My point is that no matter how much they might hate something about their current home situation, regardless of the reason why, they will grow up and out of it. They will move on. Sometimes it is parents who don't get along, maybe it's someone who deals with stress poorly, and maybe there is a lack of compassion, understanding, support or love. Maybe it is a violent house where they all live in the domestic violence cycle. Whatever the situation, they will get beyond it if they want.

The problem is, even when they are long removed from the house, deep in the filing cabinet of their mind, filed under normal is the situation they hated. I believe that when we are raised in an environment where something bad is a day-to-day norm, our sub-conscious files it away as normal or okay. As much as we hate it, if we don't safeguard ourselves against it, we will gravitate to the same activity. Just when we least expect it, maybe in an argument with our spouse or when we are tired and angry at our kids, we will find ourselves doing the same thing that we grew up hating.

Many of you know exactly what I am talking about. Many of you have found yourself thinking, "I can't believe I just did or said that. That's exactly what _____ (you fill in the blank) used to do when I was growing up and I hated it." Or you might think, "I can't believe I just treated my kid that way. That's the exact treatment I grew up hating." Or worse, "I can't believe I have two kids and I'm pregnant again, married to a man who drinks too much and hits me sometimes. I hated it when my mom and dad lived like that." It is easy for us to recognize the good traits passed on by those who raise us. Why is it hard to realize we also have some bad baggage packed away in the attic? This realization is the only way we can break the violence cycle.

In severe cases some people are so subconsciously comfortable with the violent dysfunction they grew up in, they grow uncomfortable in functional, loving relationships. They don't know why, but they become restless, unhappy and uncomfortable in normal, functional relationships and eventually end the relationship. These people often bounce from relationship to relationship, never finding happiness or security. You may know someone like this. Just when things are working out in their lives, they abruptly end the relationship and run away. A closer look at these people usually finds an extremely dysfunctional childhood.

The good news is I believe we can beat it. I believe we can rise above the baggage and ugly things filed away in our subconscious mind. The first and most important step is to be aware of it, completely. Not unlike the alcoholic who must first recognize and admit the problem, we must recognize and admit our baggage. We need to think about the dysfunction in our early households and we need to explore it completely, if only in our mind.

It is certainly best if you have a good, trusted friend to talk with about it. If you grew up in a violent household you might consider a counselor or religious mentor. Church leaders are great for this healing. Either way, all you need for them to do is listen, that's it. They only need to supply an understanding, confidential and caring ear. However you do it, you need to be aware of the baggage completely. Don't blow it off and try to pretend it never happened. But remember this, you have the responsibility to take action. It is your life and you need to work it out. It's called ownership.

My Experience

"Alcohol use, drug use, and stress do not cause domestic violence. While they may be present in violent situations, they are not the cause and are no excuse for abusive behavior."
-Choices

I really believe that if you don't deal with it, you are prone to re-live it, no matter how much you hated it. I've seen it happen and I've skirted it in my own life.

I grew up in a small southern Ohio village. I was three when my dad moved out and he and my mother were divorced. The only clear memory of my early childhood is my dad on the front steps with his suitcase packed. I asked him where he was going.

That left my mom, my sister who was a little older than me, and me, but not for long. My mom soon married my stepfather, a young man just out of the Navy. My step-dad was a construction worker. He also hunted wild game to get us through the winters when he was out of work. That's the way it was then. We didn't have the year-round construction projects of today. My mom went to school and became a beautician.

I can only imagine the tremendous stress in their lives. Money was probably always a problem, not to mention the stress of a ready made family my step-dad inherited literally over night. I remember a lot of drinking and a lot of fighting. My family has a strong history of alcoholism. Looking back, I think we lived in the domestic violence cycle, on the fast track.

I remember my step-dad moving out and back in. He almost always moved out in November and was back home by January. I suspect it was the stress of the holidays, money and otherwise. As an adult, I have had friends who fell into the same trap. Their relationship is on edge anyway and along comes the holidays with all the social and financial stress. Snap, they split up, only to be back together at the beginning of the year. I remember pointing this out to a friend while I was in the Army. He and his wife had just had their annual November split. I said, "That's interesting. That is exactly what my mom and step-dad always did." He was awestruck at the observation.

I remember many violent fights between my mom and step-dad. I remember waking up and seeing flashing police lights in my bedroom window on several occasions. I learned to roll over and go back to sleep. I remember coming downstairs in the morning and seeing the aftermath of smashed furniture. Of course, by then they were sound asleep, having been up most of the night. I remember many blow-ups, some too personal to share here. I can only imagine the hardship they endured in their lives. This went on for years.

It is amazing they remained married and led a seemingly functional life in their later years. They were alcohol free and, as an adult, it was a pleasure to visit with them. I don't harbor any ill will about my childhood. My mom and step-dad didn't have anyone to tell them why their lives were like they were, much less tell them how to change things and break the cycle.

I also recall some good things. I know my mother and step-dad did best they could with what they had. I don't know how they survived the dysfunction. Not all of us did.

Laura

In 2007, 33% of all female murder victims were killed by their husbands or boyfriends.

I believe men sometimes hide their emotional baggage better than women do. I mentioned my sister earlier. She was a couple years older than me. I clearly remember my sister being rebellious. By the time I was 13, she was 15 and ran with a bad crowd. Her grades were poor and it was only a matter of time before she was married, expecting a child, and dropped out of school.

My high school experience was much the same. Married with a child but, by the grace of God alone, I somehow managed to graduate. I was married during my senior year and didn't have to go to school if I didn't want to. Before that, having started working full-time for my uncle at his service station when I was 14, I missed a tremendous amount of school. My mom tried to keep me in school, but I was very rebellious and she had other issues she had to deal with. I only added to her problems.

After many years of struggle, my life took a turn for the better when I joined the Army National Guard in 1982. By 1985 I worked full time for the National Guard and had moved from my hometown to an apartment in Gahanna. Every couple years I changed units, which were usually located at then Rickenbacker Air National Guard Base or in the State Headquarters in Columbus. Gahanna was right in the middle.

Right now I will take the opportunity to tell any young men or women who have graduated high school, but are still trying to figure out their way in life to see their local National Guard recruiter. The Guard taught me more than I can say here, including the operational and organizational skills vital to my success in law enforcement, not to mention military discipline and bearing. It's a great place to learn and grow while waiting to see what God has in store for you.

In 1987 I was accepted as an Active Duty Soldier working for the Ohio National Guard. I was promoted quickly and even began to attend college as I could. I had long since been divorced and remarried in 1987. I have been blessed with great prosperity and joy, including a wonderful son, good employment, and good homes since then.

In 1994 I left the Guard to pursue a long sought after career in law enforcement. In eight short years I rose from patrol officer through patrol sergeant, operations sergeant, operations lieutenant and finally to the position of Deputy Chief of Police. That type of progression is unheard of in departments like mine. Because of my life experiences and education, I have always been prepared when opportunity knocked. I have been blessed beyond belief.

In 2000 I completed a Bachelor's Degree, with a 4.0 GPA, from a local business college. Not bad for a shy, skinny kid who barely made it through high school. As I said, men often hide their baggage better. My sister was not so fortunate.

My sister never seemed to rise above her struggle. Many years after her son was born, she was divorced from her first husband. Later she remarried and they had two daughters. My wife and I visited my sister often during this time and all seemed well, except for the inner-turmoil that seemed to lie just below my sister's surface. After a few years, my sister developed a relationship with a man, I'll call him the plumber, who lived with his wife and kids across the street from her. One thing led to another and soon enough my sister, along with her two daughters and son, was divorced and living with the plumber.

I didn't see my sister much after that. Her behavior was hard to understand. The only thing for certain was that her life was in turmoil. Her son became a young adult and moved out on his own. Some years passed.

Sometime in 2000, a distant cousin contacted me. My great aunt was having a birthday party and they wanted to invite my sister and me. I told them I would try to track her down, but when I asked my mom about her whereabouts, I was told my sister lived somewhere in the backwoods of Alabama. I was not surprised considering the course her life had taken. I was told the plumber decided to make a living as a professional gambler and somehow that landed them in Alabama. I've also been told the plumber was on some type of disability and never really worked a steady job the entire time he and my sister were together. Now I know the rest of the story.

On May 12, 2001 we were having a garage sale. We are not big garage sale people, but needed to clear out some of the clutter. Then came the call from my mom telling me that my sister and the plumber had become estranged and at 9:00 that morning the plumber had kicked in the door of their house and shot and killed my sister. It was unbelievable. A few days later we headed to Alabama to try to sort it all out.

It turns out my sister had been living the life of a textbook domestic violence victim. After talking with her friends, neighbors and two daughters, who by the way, were forced to witness the execution of their mother, I discovered the abuse had been the controlling, psychological kind.

The plumber had controlled and monitored every telephone conversation and personal contact my sister had with the outside world. He chimed in, belittled her, and dominated her at every turn. That is, until my sister got a job she liked and started to develop a little independence. The plumber didn't like her being gone from his sight, but he needed her income to live since his professional gambling career did little more than raid the bank account every time they were able to accumulate a little money. So much for the big time gambler. I tell young women that if any man in their life ever tells them he is quitting his job to become a professional gambler, they need to run away from him quickly and never look back.

Finally, my sister realized she didn't need him in her life and she kicked him out. At some point in the breakup, she purchased a nice home on a small piece of land from friends. It was out in the middle of nowhere, nestled on a red-clay road, but it was hers. She had achieved her high school diploma via GED and worked in a small medical facility in a nearby town. But soon enough, she let the plumber back in.

I understand she kicked him out a few times, but always let him come back. She told a friend he would stand outside the house for hours on end and peek in the windows, evidenced by the pile of cigarette butts she would find in the morning. He had also stalked her. She told friends she let him back in the house because when he lived with her at least she didn't have to constantly look over her shoulder to see where he was. The love had long since left the relationship.

I understand that the plumber was arrested once during this on-again, off-again relationship for violating some type of a protection order my sister had acquired. But, through his connections with the local government, the plumber was quickly released. I don't know the details and don't want to know at this point.

In the midst of this turmoil, my sister was really getting her life together. Her job was going well, she had many good friends, and by their own testimony, her relationship with her two teenage daughters had become the model. They both say their mom was their best friend and they were obviously a top priority in her life. She had a very nice home which she kept meticulously clean. She displayed her GED certificate proudly and had achieved additional certificates in the medical field. Things were going well, except for this controlling, domestic violence abuser that had become deeply entrenched in her life.

My sister must have seen it this way also, because then came the final break up. This time my sister changed the bank accounts so the plumber could not access her money. He knew it was finally over.

My sister knew he would not go easy. She told friends she feared for her life. She even acquired a permit from the local sheriff's department to keep a handgun with her. Her fear was that the plumber would try to run her off the road or approach her when she was in her car. She kept the pistol in the glove box of the car.

The local sheriff's detective told me that on the evening of May 11, the plumber came to my sister's house and stood outside for a while before he left. They know that from the fresh pile of cigarettes. Before he left, he pulled the phone wire out of the box on the outside of the house.

On the morning of May 12 he returned and smoked cigarettes for a while, probably building up his courage. At some point he had been to his brother's home and borrowed his brother's handgun. I'm told the plumber has a criminal history that might have prohibited him from legally purchasing a handgun.

Shortly after 9:00 am the plumber kicked in the front door and shot my sister once as she stood in the living room running the vacuum cleaner. The two daughters alerted by the loud bang, stepped into the hallway entrance to the living room. My sister said, "Don't do it," just before he fatally shot her again. He aimed the gun at the girls. The oldest said, "Don't do it." Thank God, he didn't. I guess one cold-blooded, cowardly murder was enough for the day. He lowered the gun and ran out the door.

The oldest of my nieces picked up the phone to call 911, but you already know, the line was dead. She drove down the dirt road to a friend's house to call the sheriff. They found her walking back, too distraught to drive. My sister was pronounced dead at the scene and the Alabama Bureau of Criminal Investigation was called in.

The plumber fled first to Florida and then back to Columbus, Ohio. When Gahanna detectives found he had family in the Columbus area and feared he might try to come for me, they did a full court press and actually ferreted the plumber out in Pickerington, Ohio, a community only a few miles from Gahanna, within about 10 days of the murder. It was a great example of exceptional investigative work. I had the pleasure of calling Alabama and telling my nieces, in a room full of people, that we had caught him. Until that moment, they lived in fear that he would return in the night. As I write these words over a year later, I still get chills.

My nieces moved in with their father in Columbus and the plumber is in an Alabama prison hoping for parole. Soon enough, my nieces and I will have to go back down there and testify. I am looking forward to it. I know the lies and misinformation that may be given as testimony in the parole hearing in an attempt to discredit my sister and somehow justify her brutal murder. I pray my nieces are not subjected to that. They have already seen enough.

In all the presentations I have given, one high school kid asked me if I felt any guilt over my sister's murder. I hadn't really thought about it until that moment, but I realized I do feel guilt. If I had tried to stay connected with her, I believe she would be alive today. I could have been the strong, safe haven for her when she couldn't rid herself of the plumber. I could have taken action to see that he stayed in jail the time he was arrested. As a police executive, I could have done many things. Who knows, maybe I could have convinced her to move back to Ohio where I could have provided much more protection. But, I will never know.

It's Not My Problem

"Do your boys know?
Real Men Teach Respect for Women.
Talk. Teach. Listen. Lead."
-DELTA Program Billboard

Men often turn a blind eye to this problem because they don't think it affects them. But, when you stop to realize that odds are half the women in your life - daughters, granddaughters, nieces, sisters, will become victims of some form of relationship violence in their lifetime, it becomes clear that it is everyone's problem.

When men stop to realize that the perpetrators of this violence are our sons, grandsons, nephews, and brothers, it becomes clear that men can be a key to improvement. Adult men must mentor the young men in their lives. We must lead by example and we must tell our sons and grandsons what behaviors constitute mistreatment of the women in our lives. If they don't hear it from the adult men they look up to, who will tell them?

Men need to quit laughing at the water-cooler and internet jokes about beating women. We need to have the courage to tell our friends that we find those jokes unacceptable. In short, men need to become advocates against relationship violence if we are to create a safer, better society for our daughters, granddaughters, sisters, nieces and our mothers.

Many women survive and escape the violent relationship and over the years put it out of their mind. But I find it amazing the number of women who can think back to a relationship with a man where they were either physically abused or subjected to some form of emotional abuse, maybe at the hands of a textbook controller or a boyfriend who was willing to do whatever it took to keep his girlfriend. Kicking the mirrors off her car, cutting her tires, sending threatening emails or text messages, stalking her, or performing any number of abusive acts. It is amazing to me that many young men do these things thinking that it will somehow influence the young woman to come back to him. Some young men perform these acts as punishment to the person who did the leaving.

Of course, we read frequent news reports about the women in our society who do not survive. Murder-suicide seems to be a growing trend that we read about almost weekly. We have all read and watched the news stories about the estranged, maybe divorced husband who murders every member of the family and kills himself as his last act. This is the extreme tragic escalation of a giant problem that consumes our society, but is rarely talked about.

We know that many times young men who stalk their former girlfriends escalate their actions until they get the result they want. It should be of no surprise that some men escalate their actions, all the way to murder, in their attempt to reconcile with or punish their former mate.

As a police chief of a small suburban community I start my day by reading every police report taken by our officers in the previous 24 hour period. Just this morning I read a report of an ex-husband using an old key to enter his 50 year old ex-wife's apartment and lay in wait for her return. When she came home he beat her up and held her hostage over the weekend, finally allowing her to leave Monday morning to go to work. When she returned to the house with the police by her side, the estranged husband had stolen her clothes, done significant damage to her other belongings, including pouring lighter fluid on some of her furniture, and fled. During the incident, he told her that the police could not protect her and that he would be back to kill her.

I am certain this abuser was trying hard to work up the courage to destroy everything that was hers and kill his victim. He came close while he was beating her, but stopped short, this time. I also believe he was trying to muster the courage to burn her apartment, but stopped short, this time.

It appears the victim fled her apartment and our community in an attempt to go into hiding. She believes what I believe, that her abuser will seek her out again and that by then he may have worked up the courage to complete his act.

I am sorry to say that he is probably right in his statement that the police cannot protect the victim. Our officers filed charges against the offender, an arrest warrant is on file, and we will try to find him, within the scope of our limited resources. But, if the police don't stumble across this offender and if he is as aggressive in his pursuit of this victim, as he was in abusing her and holding her hostage, he may get the opportunity to complete his act.

I am also sorry to say that this type incident is so common in our society that it will not even make the news. There will be no outcry in the local paper or on the evening news about this victim who was beaten and forced into hiding by her pursuer. It is simply so frequent in our society as a whole that it is not newsworthy.

Being a Nosey Neighbor

"Should you get involved?
He's betting you won't . . .
We hope you will."
-*Crisis Connections Campaign, Alberta, Canada*

A family within sight of my home includes two young women. I have watched these girls grow up. A couple years ago, I believe it was in the month of June, I came home from work one afternoon to see one of the young women standing on the front porch with a young man. I assumed it was her boyfriend.

I noticed right away that there was some friction in their interaction. He seemed to be trying to make up while she appeared to be trying to break up. I noticed the subtle signs that most people would have noticed. He moved forward, often prompting her to back up. He put his arms around her to hug her several times, but she did not return the hug.

I decided to be the nosey neighbor, knowing what young men can be capable of and not wanting it to happen on my watch. Further, I was compelled to practice what I preach as an advocate against relationship violence.

I stood on my front porch for almost an hour and watched, not caring that he knew I was there. Finally, I went into the house and watched from a window, prepared to make my way to her aid very quickly if required to do so.

After well over another hour had passed, the young man went to his car and left. The young woman went inside her home. I turned my attention to other things

The next day I ran into the young lady's father outside. I told him about my observations and concerns. He told me that his daughter had been dating this guy on and off for a long time and that was just how their relationship went, there was nothing to worry about.

Several days after the incident I saw the girl's mother in her driveway. I told her about my observations and concerns. She told me the boy was a nice kid and that her daughter was more than capable of taking care of herself. I apologized for being a nosey neighbor and said it must just be a cop thing.

About mid-November of the same year, almost five months after observing the interaction on the neighbor's front porch, the young lady's father saw me in my driveway and came over to talk to me. He asked me if his daughter had talked with me yet. I told him she had not. He promptly retrieved the young women from their home to come out and speak with me.

It turned out that the she had broken up with the boyfriend during that June interaction on the front porch, but as is all too often the case, the young man had not given up easily. He had continued to send daily text messages, emails, and voicemail messages and had even followed her to restaurants and reported back to her via voice mail messages on her cell phone.

My neighbor's daughter had a new boyfriend and the old boy friend was engaged in full-blown stalking. In fact, while she was telling me the story, the old boyfriend texted her and called her phone several times. Five months later and this guy was escalating his behavior.

She asked me what she should do. I did not hesitate to tell her that she needed to call the police immediately. I actually made the call for her. While we were waiting for the police, I told her that once he knew that she had completed a police report to expect the former boyfriend to tell the police that it was her who had been stalking him. This is a textbook response by young men when their behavior is exposed to the light of day. Even though the victim had evidence in the form of text messages, email messages, and voicemail messages, these offenders still convince themselves that they are not the bad guy in the entire thing.

I also told my neighbor that the boyfriend was probably in the neighborhood watching us at that exact time. This is a typical activity of young men consumed with obsessive behavior over a former girlfriend. He had already demonstrated his inclination to stalk his victim by previously following her and her new boyfriend to a restaurant.

The police officer arrived and asked the young lady to come to the police department, just a few blocks away, to complete the report and file charges. On the way to the police department, she passed the former boyfriend. Sure enough, he had been in the neighborhood.

The offender probably watched his victim enter the police department, because she had not been inside long when he called to speak to the police sergeant taking the report on the incident.

The wise sergeant told him to come to the police department to tell his story. He was there within minutes. The police sergeant promptly arrested him for menacing by stalking, a crime in Ohio.

While the offender was in jail, I told my neighbor that upon his release from jail and pending his court hearing to be prepared for one of two textbook responses to being arrested for his activity. Either he would come out of jail set on escalating his behavior further, maybe even seeking to commit violence to her property or to her person or that being arrested would be the significant emotional event required to jolt him to his senses and that she would never hear from him again.

I warned her to be vigilant, keep her eyes open, know her surroundings, always be ready to call the police if need be, etc., all the things we tell people to do when there might be someone out there who wants to do them harm.

Fortunately, in this case, the boyfriend got out of jail and the young lady never heard from him again. The arrest was his wake-up call. Unfortunately, this is rarely the case. All too often simply being arrested and spending a few nights in jail is not the significant emotional event required to change abusive, menacing, and stalking behavior.

Stop the Cycle

"He beat her 150 times.
She only got flowers once."
-National Coalition Against Domestic Violence

In closing, I tell young women to never accept anything less than 100% respect from the men in their lives. I plead with them to never take that first step down the path of tolerance.   Regardless of the gain, the consequences are not worth it.

A local minister summed it up in a recent sermon when he said, "Women are very loving and compassionate. They tend to tolerate many shortcomings in the men in their lives, believing they can change or 'fix' their men. It's okay to be compassionate and loving, but in situations where men are violent, get away. Don't try to fix them and don't try to change them.   Terminate the relationship and get away early. At the first hint of any type of relationship violence, drop them quickly and leave them to their own devices."

I tell young women to not only terminate the relationship at the first hint of controlling or violent behavior, but to make sure everyone knows about it.   Tell your parents, friends and, if need be, the local police.

Leave no doubt in anyone's mind why you have cut the offender from your life. It's his problem. He is responsible to fix it.

I also tell the men in the audience that if they ever experience any violent tendencies towards anyone in their household or relationships to seek help and get it fixed within themselves before it ruins their life. I tell young men that if they have strong urges to physically strike out when they are frustrated or angry, to speak with a trusted school or religious counselor about it and get it fixed. I speak to the alarming trend of domestic violence calls where the teenage son is fighting the mother. This is an unacceptable trend that must stop. The solution lies with young men taking responsibility and breaking the cycle.

Finally, I remind the entire audience of their tendency to be violent if they were raised in a violent home. I remind them of their responsibility to break the cycle of relationship violence.

Relationship violence is a plague on our society that has been around forever. Nothing I can say or do can end the plague, but if I can change just one life, if I can convince just one man or women to change their course away from the violence, I have been successful. We must stop the cycle.

Police Officer on a Mission for Dead Sister

BARBARA CARMEN
The Columbus Dispatch, Sunday, May 25, 2003

Laura Jo Moore was killed in the backwoods of Alabama. But she is far from silenced. Stalked and shot by an abusive husband, Laura is remembered here in her hometown, where her story is a warning for teenagers.

"I speak on behalf of my sister."
Larry Rinehart begins.

The anguish in his voice draws in the kids. This guy has credentials. He is a grieving brother. He is also deputy chief of police in Gahanna. Often, as he talks, he'll see boys avoid his gaze, or girls nod and whisper. Direct hit. Other times, a thin voice will stop him afterward in a hallway: "Please, I need some advice." Rinehart grabs at these second chances to help. He did not know of Laura's abuse. Her isolation was a warning signal. Larance Moore had moved his wife and her two daughters from suburban Columbus to a clay-road junction in Lawley, Alabama. "The middle of nowhere," Rinehart said in an interview. In his pamphlet for students, "Relationship Violence,"

Rinehart describes his sister's life with her third husband: "He monitored every telephone conversation and personal contact my sister had with the outside world. He chimed in, belittled her, and dominated her at every turn."

As he discovered details of Laura's murder, he began to stitch together similarities between that abuse and what he had seen on the street.

"This is an affluent suburb. Yet when I first came, I was shocked at some of the things I heard boys call their girlfriends in front of other boys. The girls just took it."

"Let me clue you in, girls: When a guy calls you a streetwalker — or worse — it is not a tender expression of love, but a glimpse of rage."

"This name-calling is a first step on the path of tolerance," Rinehart said.

Guys may think they're being cool, imitating rap songs or movies, but such behavior desensitizes teens and primes them to accept later abuse.

"I tell the boys that I'm not male bashing. I'm a member of that brotherhood. But in our culture, 95 percent of the victims are female."

He tells girls to stop trying to fix their guys. Get away, and fast.

Rinehart is "a real find," said Karen S. Days, executive director of the Columbus Coalition Against Family Violence. He spoke last year to 350 teens at a coalition workshop.

"Afterward, all the kids just gathered around him," she said. "It was amazing. His story, the story of his sister, is so important to tell."

On May 12, 2001, Laura's third husband stood outside his wife's tidy, prefab home and chain-smoked. Laura, 44, had filed for divorce, but her husband decided to end the marriage on his terms. He kicked open the front door and shot her dead as his stepdaughters watched in terror.

Unbelievably, an Alabama judge this month sentenced Moore to life in prison — then allowed the possibility of parole after 10 years. The daughters have returned to central Ohio to live with their father, Laura's second husband. They are safe. They have a loving family. But they have lost a mother. Who will help them pick out a wedding gown, or provide advice when the baby has colic? Laura was a great role model. Despite her abuse, she'd earned her GED, taken advanced courses and secured a solid job as a medical technician. Laura even had managed to buy the tiny house. She also bought a pistol, but she kept it in her car. She thought she'd be safe in her own home. Last week, Rinehart took Laura's story to the Statehouse. "Criminals carry guns, and they don't give a hoot about what goes on in these chambers," Rinehart told a Senate panel considering a proposed concealed-carry gun law. "Those law-abiding citizens deserve a right to arm themselves." That's powerful stuff coming from a cop who often sees violent relationships erupt. Gahanna police responded to 215 domestic calls last year. "We've got to stop the cycle," he said. He is trying. Rinehart could not save his sister. But I'll bet he saves a stranger.

Identifying Relationship Violence

The Red Flags

Using Intimidation

- Making threatening looks, actions, or gestures
- Smashing things in front of you and/or destroying property
- Hurting your pet(s)
- Displaying weapons

Using Emotional Abuse

- Humiliating you through insults, name-calling, shaming, and public put-downs
- Playing mind games in an effort to make you think you're crazy
- Making you feel guilty about the abuse

Using Isolation

- Increasing your dependence on him by limiting your outside involvements/activities

- Controlling what you do, who you see and talk to, what you read, and where you go
- Using jealousy as an excuse to justify abusive behaviors

Minimizing, Denying, and Blaming

- Making light of the abuse or denying that it has occurred
- Shifting responsibility for the abuse onto you
- Making excuses for inexcusable behavior

Using Children

- Making you feel guilty about involving the children
- Using children to relay messages
- Threatening to take the children away
- Using visitation time to harass you

Using Male Privilege

- Treating you like a servant, a child, or his possession
- Expecting you to obey him without question
- Acting like "master of the castle"
- Making all family decisions without your input

Using Economic Abuse

- Preventing you from getting or keeping a job
- Making you ask for money or giving you an allowance
- Taking your money

- Preventing your knowledge of or access to family income

Using Coercion and Threats

- Making and/or carrying out threats to hurt you

- Threatening to hurt or kill you, your children, other family members, or even pets

- Threatening to leave you, commit suicide, or report you to child protective services

- Forcing you to do illegal things

- Making you drop charges against him

If you are involved in a relationship where you are being hurt or abused, remember that you are not alone, it is not your fault, and help is available. Call the CHOICES 24-hour hotline at (614) 224-4663.

www.choicescolumbs.org

Types of Relationship Violence

It's not just physical.

Emotional/Psychological Abuse

Emotional or psychological abuse involves any behavior, verbal or non-verbal, that negatively impacts another person's emotional or psychological well-being. Examples include:

- Name-calling, mocking, yelling, swearing
- Making humiliating remarks or gestures
- Telling you what to do, where you can and cannot go, or monitoring your activities
- Putting you down in front of other people
- Saying negative things about or preventing you from seeing your friends and family
- Cheating or being overly jealous
- Shifting responsibility for abusive behavior by blaming others or saying you caused it

Economic Abuse

When money becomes a tool by which the abuser can further control the victim, economic abuse is occurring. Examples of economic abuse include:

- Denying you all access to funds

- Having to account for every penny spent
- Putting all bills in your name
- Demanding your paychecks
- Interfering with your work or not letting you work
- Taking your car keys or otherwise preventing you from using the car

Physical Abuse

Physical abuse is the easiest to recognize and understand than other types of abuse. Physical abuse is:

- Scratching, biting, grabbing, or spitting
- Shoving, pushing, slapping, or punching
- Throwing objects or destroying possessions or treasured objects
- Refusing to help you when you are sick, injured, pregnant, or if you are physically disabled
- Threatening or attacking with a weapon
- Stabbing, burning, or strangling
- Attempting to kill you

Sexual Abuse

Sexual abuse can be defined as any sexual encounter without consent and includes the following:

- Being forced to participate in unwanted, unsafe or degrading sexual activities
- Denying you contraception or protection against sexually transmitted diseases
- Sexual exploitation through photography or prostitution

Abuse in Later Life

Abuse in later life occurs when an older person is subjected to a pattern of coercive behaviors used to gain and maintain power and control. It is most often perpetrated by a family member or someone with whom the elder has an ongoing relationship. This type of abuse is characterized by:

- Emotional and psychological abuse
- Threats of physical violence or abandonment
- Isolation from family and friends
- Financial exploitation
- Denial of healthcare access

While women of all ages face similar issues when trying to leave an abuser, older women face additional, unique challenges. Many of these women grew up and married during a time when domestic abuse was often ignored. Now, at an older age, they have suffered many years of abuse and may have developed a poor self-image and feelings of shame. Additionally:

- An older woman who has been abused is less likely to tell anyone about it
- She may be facing health problems that keep her dependent on her abuser
- She may feel obligated and/or committed to caring for her abusive aging partner
- She may be afraid of being alone

If you are involved in a relationship where you are being hurt or abused, remember that you are not alone, it is not your fault, and help is available. Call the CHOICES 24-hour hotline at (614) 224-4663.

Teen Dating Violence

It shouldn't hurt to be in love.

Dating abuse occurs when harmful behaviors are repeated, creating a pattern of violence. **Physical abuse** occurs when a teen is pinched, hit, shoved, or kicked. **Emotional abuse** means threatening a teen or harming his or her sense of self-worth. Examples include name-calling, teasing, threats, bullying, or keeping a teen away from friends and family. **Sexual abuse** is forcing a teen to engage in a sex act. This includes fondling and rape.

Dating abuse often starts with teasing and name-calling. These behaviors are often thought to be a "normal" part of a relationship. But they can lead to more serious abuse, like physical assault and rape.

Does your boyfriend/girlfriend:

- Look at you or act in ways that scare you?

- Act jealous or possessive?

- Put you down or criticize you?

- Try to control where you go, what you wear or what you do?

- Text or IM you excessively?

- Blame you for the hurtful things they say and do?

- Threaten to kill or hurt you or themselves if you leave them?

- Try to stop you from seeing or talking to friends and family?

- Try to force you to have sex before you're ready?

- Do they hit, slap, push or kick you?

If you are a teen involved in a relationship where you are being hurt or abused, remember that you are not alone, it is not your fault, and help is available. Contact the National Teen Dating Abuse Hotline at (866) 331-9474 or visit **loveisnotabuse.com**.

You can also contact CHOICES for information about our STAR (Supportive Talk About Relationships) teen support group by calling (614) 224-4663.

What To Do To Stay Safe

End the Silence.
It is everybody's business.

Below are tips to help keep you as safe as possible. Following these suggestions can't guarantee your safety, but they could help make you safer.

Call the Police

If at any time you feel you are in danger from your abuser, you can call 911 or the local police. In some instances, CHOICES can provide you with a cell phone that is programmed to only call 911. These pre-programmed phones are for use only when you need to contact the police and you are unable to use any other phone. Contact us at (614) 224-4663 for more information. If you do contact the police, consider the following information. Your participation will help the police do their job more efficiently, which will help your efforts to stay safe.

- If your abuser is still present when the police arrive, ask to speak with them in private.

- When the police arrive, tell them in detail what happened leading up to you making the call, including everything your abuser said and did.

- If your abuser hit you, tell the police where, how many times you were hit, and show them any marks that are left on your body. Not all marks will show up immediately. If you see marks after the police are gone, call the police to have pictures taken of the marks. The pictures may be used in court.

- If your abuser has broken any property, show the police exactly what has been damaged.

- If you and your children choose not to stay in the home, the police can help you leave safely.

- The police can give you information on domestic violence programs and shelters, like those at CHOICES.

- The police are required to make a report documenting what happened to you. Police reports can be used in court if your abuser is charged with a crime. A police report can also be used to help you get a protection order against your abuser.

- Get the officers' names, badge numbers, and the report number in case you need a copy of the report.

Get Support from Family, Friends, and Co-Workers

Discuss your situation with friends, family, and co-workers who are supportive of you. Maintaining regular contact with people who support you is crucial to helping you stay safe, whether you're at home or at work.

If you decide to stay in your home and in your relationship, ask a friend or family member to help you develop a **safety plan**, which includes setting aside money and important documents in a safe place, as well as making a plan to leave.

If you do decide to leave the relationship, friends and family can help you make that transition. They may be able to help you with finding financial assistance, finding a new place to live, storing your belongings, or getting help from a domestic violence program like CHOICES.

Find a Safe Place to Stay

While you may not feel that leaving your home is fair, sometimes leaving is the only way to ensure that you stay safe. If staying with family or friends is not an option, contact CHOICES at (614) 224-4663 for information about **temporary emergency shelter** and other programs.

Get Medical Attention

If your abuser has hurt you, seek immediate medical attention from your doctor or the hospital. It is very important to give as much information about your injuries as you feel comfortable sharing. Keep in mind:

- You may have injuries you can't see or are not aware of

- What appears to be a minor injury could, in fact, be serious

- If you are pregnant and were hit in your stomach, tell the doctor immediately

- Because abusers often hit their victims in the head, domestic violence victims can be in danger of closed head injuries. If you experience any of these symptoms, get medical care immediately: memory loss, dizziness, vision problems, vomiting, long-lasting headaches.

- If your abuser held you by the throat and your breathing was interrupted, tell the doctor immediately.

Safety During a Violent Incident

It's not just physical.

Go to an area that has an exit.

Not a bathroom (near hard surfaces), kitchen (knives), or near weapons.

Stay in a room with a phone.

Call 911, a friend or a neighbor, if possible. Inform them if there are weapons in the home.

In some instances, CHOICES can provide you with a cell phone that is programmed to only call 911. These pre-programmed phones are for use only when you need to contact the police and you are unable to use any other phone. Contact us at (614) 224-4663 for more information.

Know your escape route.

Practice how to get out of your home safely. Visualize your escape route.

Have a packed bag ready.

Keep it hidden in a handy place in order to leave quickly, or leave the bag elsewhere if the abuser searches your home.

Devise a code word or signal.

Tell your children, grandchildren or neighbors so you can communicate to them that you need the police.

Know where you're going.

Plan where you will go if you have to leave home, even if you don't think you'll need to.

Trust your judgment.

Consider anything that you feel will keep you safe and give you time to figure out what to do next. Sometimes it is best to flee, at other times it may be better to calm down the abuser - anything that works to protect you and the children.

Be an Advocate.

Stay knowledgable on this problem by contacting these organizations and more:

The Family Violence Coalition
The Center for Family Safety and Healing
www.CCAFV.org
614-722-5985

CHOICES Eliminating Domestic Violence
www.choicescolumbus.org
24 hr crisis line/shelter 614-224-4663
Administrative number: 614-224-7200

ASHA – Ray of Hope
www.asharayofhope.org
Crisis Line: 614-565-2918
614-326-2121

ACTION OHIO Coalition For Battered Women
www.actionohio.org
E-mail: actionohio@sbcglobal.net
614- 825-0551

About the Author

Larry Rinehart served 12 years in the Ohio Army National Guard from 1982 to 1994. He left full-time employment in the Guard in 1994 to pursue a career in law enforcement.

Rinehart joined the Gahanna Police Department and during the next 13 years served as a Community Police Officer, Bicycle Officer, SWAT Officer, Patrol Sergeant, Operations Sergeant, Operations Lieutenant, Public Information Officer, and Deputy Chief of Police.

In 2002, Chief Rinehart completed his Bachelors Degree in Organizational Management and Leadership Techniques and Human Resource Management. In 2004 he completed his Masters Degree in Business Administration (MBA) with a focus on government and nonprofit organizations. Chief Rinehart was the recipient of the 2004 Choices Peacemaker award for his efforts against domestic and relationship violence. He was selected as the Chief of Police for the City of Bexley in April of 2007.

Chief Rinehart is an energetic and enthusiastic instructor and lecturer and often provides public speaking presentations on the topics of family and relationship violence, personal safety and awareness, workplace violence, and leadership and organizational challenges. Much of his published writing is a product of his teaching and speaking notes.

Magnanimous in nature, Rinehart is constantly sought out by neighbors, friends, bystanders and colleagues for advice and empathy on all these topics. He genuinely concerns himself with the details of their dilemmas and stories, and is warmly regarded within the community.

– Word Spigot Publishing

Made in the USA
Middletown, DE
13 September 2016